WORKING OUT THE COVENANT

THE JOURNEY SO FAR

Peter Thompson

Published by
Church of Ireland Publishing
Church of Ireland House
Church Avenue
Rathmines, Dublin 6

www.cip.ireland.anglican.org

Designed by Susan Hood

ISBN 978-1-904884-16-3

Printed by Paceprint Trading Ltd,
Dublin, Ireland

Table of Contents

Further details of the ongoing work of the Covenant
Council, and all
documents can be accessed through the Council's
website:
http://www.covenantcouncil.com/

Preface

AS CO-CHAIRS OF THE Covenant Council of the Church of Ireland and the Methodist Church in Ireland, it gives us great pleasure to commend this short history of the 'special' relationship between our two Churches to our clergy and people. We are most grateful to the Revd Peter Thompson, who has compiled this booklet on behalf of the Covenant Council, adapting material from his thesis from the Irish School of Ecumenics.

As we journey forward together in the spirit of the Covenant, it is our hope that this booklet will go some way to helping us to understand the closeness of our historic links as sister churches, and the greatness of our shared heritage of history, spirituality and liturgy. It is hoped that this will be the first in a series of publications by the Covenant Council which seek to enlarge our understanding one of the other.

Our divided family is being drawn toward fuller communion by our common heritage and our desire to be faithfully together in worship, mission and witness. Ultimately it is the Holy Spirit who calls us into a bold and new journey towards visible unity.

✠ Harold, Down & Dromore
Revd David Kerr

1
Introduction

THE AGEING JOHN WESLEY intertwined two beech saplings at Chrome Hill, Lambeg, Lisburn, saying as he did so, that this was how he hoped the church (of England, Ireland), and 'the people called Methodist' would be – in relationship with each other and growing side by side. Sadly, this vision was not fulfilled in the histories and lives of the two churches. The churches have much in common, and with the impetus of the developing ecumenical movement in the twentieth century, they have been in a position to move closer to Wesley's ideal at local, national and international levels.

This short history has been compiled on behalf of the Covenant Council of the Church of Ireland and Methodist Church in Ireland to raise awareness of the length and depth of the historical links between our two churches. It is not a comprehensive history of either church, but focuses solely on the historical connections between them both.

The bulk of the first four chapters comes from *Methodist-Anglican dialogue in Ireland 1989-2003; The work of the Joint Theological Working Party*, an MPhil thesis by the Revd Peter Thompson, presented to the Irish School of Ecumenics, and the final chapter is from *Dialogue for the sake of mission*, a paper presented to the Oxford Institute of Methodist Studies in 2002 by Gillian Kingston.

Particular thanks must be expressed to several people who have assisted in the production of this booklet:

the Revd Canon Kenneth Kearon who supervised the original research for the thesis whilst Director of the Irish School of Ecumenics; Mrs Gillian Kingston and the Revd Donald Ker for proofreading, correcting and providing many helpful suggestions; the co-chairs and secretary of the Covenant Council for their encouragement and assistance; the Irish School of Ecumenics, under whose auspices the original thesis was produced; and the librarians and staff of the RCB and ISE libraries in Dublin, who provided much valuable assistance in locating obscure documents.

We are deeply indebted to Dr Susan Hood for editing this booklet and designing the layout, and for all in Church of Ireland Publishing for their expertise and assistance in making it available to both our Churches.

2
A History of Methodism

Introduction to eighteenth-century Anglicanism

THE LATE SEVENTEENTH AND early eighteenth centuries were a time of spiritual awakening and growth in the Church of England. This was evidenced particularly by the growth of religious societies within the church, some of which have survived to this day, including the Society for the Propagation of Christian Knowledge (SPCK). The overall aim of the majority of these societies was to foster and develop the spiritual lives of their members. These societies were one of the tangible symptoms of the evangelical revival of the eighteenth century, from which John Wesley emerged as one of the most significant leaders.

The Wesleys, The Holy Club and early societies

John Wesley's father (Samuel) and grandfather (also John) were both priests of the Church of England. His grandfather was one of 2000 priests who were forced to leave the Church of England in what is known as the Great Ejectment, following their refusal to subscribe to the Act of Uniformity (to the Book of Common Prayer) in 1662. He worked as a dissenting minister for his remaining years. His son, Samuel, born in the year of the Great Ejectment, returned to the Church of England, being ordained priest in 1689 and holding livings in South Ormsby in Lincolnshire, and Epworth in North Lincolnshire.

John Wesley's mother, Susanna, was a daughter of the

Revd Dr Samuel Annesley, also a dissenting minister. Like her husband, Susanna Wesley rejoined the Church of England. A cultured and educated woman, she taught her children at home; she made a point of spending time every week with each individual child. She had a formative influence on John Wesley.

Of the 19 children born to Samuel and Susanna Wesley, three boys and seven girls survived to adulthood, and all three of the boys were ordained to the priesthood in the Church of England.

John Wesley studied at Oxford, and was elected to a fellowship there. After two years as his father's curate he returned to the College, where his brother Charles had formed a small society with some other undergraduates. The group studied the Bible and other Christian books, carefully observed the feasts and fasts of the Church and practised works of charity. This group received several nicknames, including Bible Moths, the Holy Club, the Godly Club, Sacramentarians, the Reforming Club, Supererogationists and Methodists, the latter a jibe at their methodical approach to the Christian faith and lifestyle. Several of the members of the group went on to become leaders of the evangelical revival.

In March 1739 George Whitefield, an evangelist working in the west of England and sometime member of the Holy Club in Oxford, invited Wesley to assist him in his work. He convinced Wesley of the value of field preaching, a method which Wesley considered vile. The industrial revolution had seen a huge demographic shift towards larger urban centres. The parish system was geared towards smaller agricultural communities, and felt a strain with this shift. The labourers were not seen as acceptable in the fashionable churches in towns, and it was to these labourers that the field preachers, and hence the Methodists, went. Thus the origins of Methodism in England were essentially working class.[1] From societies based in Bristol and London Wesley began to journey around these islands on preaching tours and organising Methodist societies. It is important at this point to remember that these were still societies within the Established Church and were formed to encourage the spiritual lives of members, to promote holiness and its outworking in the social gospel. An important aspect of this was that members of Methodist societies were expected to attend their local parish church to receive Holy Communion at least monthly and to attend Morning and Evening Prayer on other Sundays in addition to their Methodist meetings.

Early Methodists in Ireland

The first preacher to come to Ireland was the Revd George Whitefield, whose chance visit was caused by a shipwreck on his return from America in 1738. While in Ireland he visited Dublin, was entertained by the dean of St Patrick's and the archbishop of Armagh, and preached in St Werburgh's and St Andrew's.[2] He made no attempt to follow up this work and did not return to Ireland until 1751.[3] Following the Williamite wars in Ireland during the later part of the seventeenth century there were almost 15,000 English soldiers garrisoned throughout

Ireland. Among these were many Methodists, and when they discovered no Methodist societies in the areas in which they were garrisoned they founded their own. The first preacher sent by Wesley was one Thomas Williams, who arrived in Dublin early in the year 1747. Wesley himself visited Ireland for the first time in August of that year. On Sunday 9th August, his first afternoon in Dublin, he preached in St Mary's.[4] However Archbishop Charles Cobbe would not allow a field preacher to occupy a pulpit in his diocese, and Wesley never again preached in a Church of Ireland Church in the diocese under the four successive archbishops to Cobbe. In 1789 he was invited to assist in the administration of the Holy Communion in St Patrick's Cathedral, Dublin, but not to preach. Wesley visited Ireland 21 times, at first annually, and latterly bi-annually, visiting all counties except Kerry and Roscommon. In the 42 years to 1789, membership of Methodist societies rose to 14,000.

There was much opposition to the Methodists in the form of sermons and pamphlets by clergy of the Church of Ireland. Cooney observes three reasons for this hostility: (1) a fear of enthusiasm (an excess of feeling and emotion). Enthusiasm was a major fear of the Church of England in the eighteenth century, particularly that it could inflame people to fanaticism, and plunge the country again into religious strife. Enthusiasm was the antithesis of reason; (2) the adverse reflection on the zeal of the clergy, and (3) some preachers were not as unfaltering as Wesley in their loyalty and affection for the Established Church.[5]

The seeds of separation

Throughout his life Wesley never ceased to protest his loyalty to the Established Church, although it was through some of his own actions in later years that separation became inevitable. The primary one was the ordination (for service in America) of several of his preachers in 1784. Methodist societies in America numbered some 15,000 members, and many were independent of the Church of England, for the same reasons as they had fought for political independence from Britain. The consequence of this separation was that they had no access to the sacraments, because they had no presbyters. At this time Methodists were still a group within the Church of England and attended the Established Church to receive the sacraments. Following the break with the Church of England, Wesley approached the Bishop of London to ordain one of the Methodist preachers for America. After the bishop's refusal, and having read, amongst other works Stillingfleet's *Irenicum*, Hooker's *Laws of ecclesiastical polity book VII*, and King's *Enquiry* and *Account of the Primitive Church*, Wesley became convinced that bishops and priests were of the same order. The basic argument was that, from close study of the New Testament, the words *episcopos* and *presbuteros* appear to be used interchangeably for those in a position of oversight within the churches, and it was only in post apostolic times that the hierarchical structures came to be developed. In September 1784, assisted by two other Anglican priests, Wesley ordained two men deacons and then presbyters to serve in America, and one of his assistants, Thomas Coke, as superintendent. On arrival in America, the three men proceeded to ordain

Francis Asbury, the leading preacher there, as deacon, elder and superintendent. They went on to organise the Methodist Episcopal Church, with Coke and Asbury as bishops. This was the first occasion when a Methodist body claimed to be a Church. Between 1785 and 1787 Wesley ordained 11 more for work in Scotland, Canada and the West Indies. In 1788 he ordained the first priest for work in England and three more the following year. The relationship between priest and bishop in the Anglican and Methodist understandings remains as perhaps the most major issue in the current dialogue and is the primary issue that all documents at national[6] and international[7] levels identify for further dialogue.

In 1784, the year when he ordained the first presbyters, Wesley said: 'I believe I shall not separate from the Church of England until my soul separates from my body',[8] and only three years later he said 'when Methodists leave the Church, God will leave them'.[9] The Deed of Declaration[10] was also signed in 1784, giving Methodism an independent legal status, and taking a step in turning it from a society into a Church. Towards the end of his life Wesley acknowledged that Methodism had developed to a point where the Church of England could no longer contain it. He maintained that he had only done what had to be done, and regretted the separation. He explained the tension between his two principles as 'The one, I dare not separate from the Church, that I believe it would be a sin to do so; the other, that I believe it would be a sin not to vary from it in... cases of necessity'.[11]

Wesley viewed separation as ceasing to attend services. He did not see the ordinations as constituting separation.

At this time Methodist meetings were held in the early morning (usually at 5am), and the evening, so that members could attend both the morning and evening services in the Established Church in addition to the Methodist meetings. Wesley was concerned that they should experience a balance of liturgy and preaching. In 1788 Thomas Coke arrived in Dublin and discovered that many Methodists were attending dissenting meetings on Sundays instead of the Established Church. This he regarded as unacceptable. To curtail the practice, Coke arranged that on three Sundays out of four, Methodist services would be held in the Whitefriar Street chapel at the same time as the dissenting meetings (and by implication at the same time as those of the Established Church). At these services, the Book of Common Prayer was to be used, and on the first Sunday of the month the people were to attend Holy Communion in St Patrick's Cathedral, or their local parish church. At first Wesley over-ruled this arrangement, but later conceded. When he conceded, he observed that they no longer attended dissenting meetings and 'that three times more went to St Patrick's... in six or twelve months than had done for ten or twenty years before. Observe! This is done not to *prepare for* but to *prevent* a separation from the Church'.[12] Jeffrey comments that in St Patrick's Cathedral, there are still 'outsize Communion vessels which had to be provided towards the end of the eighteenth century on account of the very large number of

Methodists who attended Communion services'.[13]

In 1795, four years after Wesley's death, the Plan of Pacification allowed for the administration of the sacraments in certain Methodist chapels, and this is usually seen as the point where Methodism in Great Britain parted from the Established Church. The Plan of Pacification stated that where there was a demand for the sacraments to be administered by preachers, and where the trustees at one meeting, and the stewards and leaders at another agreed to it, subject also to the approval conference, permission could be then granted to specified preachers. It was an acknowledgement that many people had lost any real connection with the Church of England (if indeed they ever had such a connection) and that they should not be asked to attend its services. This did not apply to Ireland, where the separation did not occur for a further 20 years. At the Irish Conference in 1795, there were requests to allow for the administration of the sacraments, but they were refused, to maintain links with the Church of Ireland. The following year, three preachers were disciplined for administering the sacraments. Two further petitions submitted in 1798 led to the expulsion of 32 leaders of the Lisburn circuit. The next discussion was in 1812, and in 1815 the Revd Adam Averell, who had been ordained a Church of Ireland deacon, but never priest, was allowed to administer the Holy Communion in as many places as possible. At the 1816 Conference, eight preachers were disciplined for administering the Communion, but yielding to demand, the Conference permitted the Communion to be administered in eight circuits, and this permission soon became general.

Irish Methodism splits

As a reaction to this decision, a Conference was con-
vened on 2 October 1816 at Clones for those who
wished to retain the traditional links with the Church
of Ireland. Irish Methodism had effectively split in
two. Those present at the Clones Conference believed
that in following the sacramental practice of Wesley
they were his true heirs. When their constitution was
drafted the following January, they chose the name
'The Primitive Wesleyan Methodist Society',[14] and
chose the Revd Adam Averell as President.
Membership of the Wesleyan Methodists in 1816 was
numbered at 28,542, dropping to 19,052 in 1818. The
Primitive Wesleyan membership in that year numbered 8,095. In 1821 the Wesleyans numbered 23,538
and the Primitive Wesleyans 13,563, reflecting an overall increase in Methodist membership of 8,000 since
1814.[15]

When the wheels which led to the disestablishment of
the Church of Ireland in 1871 began turning in 1868,
the Primitive Wesleyan Society was forced to question
its existence. Its function was to maintain Methodist
societies as an evangelical group within the
Established Church, but now there was no
Established Church. They were facing the additional
problem of rapidly declining membership. In 1869 the
Wesleyan Conference approached them with a proposal to reunite, but this revealed a division among the
Primitive Wesleyans, some of whom retained loyalties

to the Church of Ireland. Some members of the Primitive Wesleyan Conference met unofficially with members of the Church of Ireland to discuss their integration into the parochial system. This was followed by several official meetings. However, the Church of Ireland was not prepared to accept the administration of the sacraments by preachers who were lay-men, or the stationing of preachers by Conference, over which bishops had no power. The Church of Ireland would not abandon episcopal authority and the Primitives would not accept it. The Primitives were also worried about the effects of the Oxford Movement, specifically the increased ritualism which was becoming prevalent in the Church of Ireland. The minutes of their Conference of 1870 describe their fears:

> Men who have been educated in our universities, who have obtained Divinity Testimonials, and who have entered the sacred office of the Ministry are now openly propagating Romish and anti-scriptural errors.[16]

In 1877, the Conferences of the Wesleyan Methodists and the Primitive Wesleyans had approved the terms of union, which was effected the following year. Thus was born the Methodist Church in Ireland, and with it were broken all formal links with the Church of Ireland. As a result both Churches suffered losses: the Church of Ireland suffered a narrowing of its theological spectrum by the loss of so many evangelicals, and the Methodists an impoverishment in worship.

3
Methodist–Anglican Dialogue in Great Britain

IN 1920, THE LAMBETH CONFERENCE'S 'An appeal to all Christian people',[17] provided the first opportunity for talks between the Church of England and the Free Churches. It acknowledged the fundamental unity of all Christians through baptism and proposed a slightly adapted form of the Lambeth Quadrilateral of 1888 as the basis for further visible unity. These talks broke down because of the insistence of the need of episcopal ordination for all the Free Church ministers. Specific Anglican-Methodist dialogue can trace its roots to archbishop Fisher's Cambridge sermon of 1946, where he appealed to the Free Churches to consider taking 'episcopacy into their system' This led to the multilateral report of 1950, *Church relations in England*. The Methodist Church was the only Church to respond positively, and this led to the Anglican-Methodist conversations and the failed unity proposal of 1972. The 1950 report identified common ground on fundamental Christian doctrine, based on the Scriptures and the ecumenical creeds. In subsequent talks it was felt that there were no major doctrinal differences, and common statements on baptism and the Eucharist were agreed.

Regarding the ministry, they deployed the idea of a representative priesthood, whilst also affirming the corporate priesthood of all believers. They concluded that the views of priesthood and ministry expressed in the historic formularies of the Church of England included within their limits the understanding held by the Methodist Church. The talks also concluded that 'the historic episcopate was not the only channel of sacramental grace and true doctrine, nor a guarantee of it'.[18] They acknowledged the reality of a corporately exercised *episkope* in the Methodist Church. The proposed scheme of reunion in 1972 received the required majority of 75% in the Methodist Conference, but the General Synod failed to reach this majority.

In 1972 the Church of England extended Eucharistic hospitality to baptised communicant members of other Churches, following the recommendation of the Lambeth Conference of 1968,[19] and there was also a growth in co-operation with other churches, especially the Methodist Church. In 1982 a 'Covenanting for unity' proposal which involved the United Reformed and Moravian Churches in addition to the Methodist Church was brought before the General Synod. This also did not reach the requisite majority. In 1994 overtures were instigated by the Methodist Church, which led to informal conversations in 1995-96, and ultimately to the signing of the English Covenant.

4
The Irish Dialogue

THE LAMBETH 'APPEAL' OF 1920 led to the foundation of the United Council of Christian Churches and Religious Communions in Ireland including Presbyterians, Methodists and Anglicans. The Council was the first significant landmark for dialogue in Ireland, but it did not, however, discuss doctrinal issues, or propose any further moves towards reunion. The first moves toward this had come in the form of the 1917 report of the joint co-operation committee of the Presbyterian and Methodist Churches in Ireland which had recommended the formation of a council of churches. This was based on the suggestion of the Rt. Revd Charles D'Arcy, then bishop of Down, Connor and Dromore (1911-19), in the February edition of *The Spectator* of the same year.

The General Assembly of the Presbyterian Church in 1919 proposed a resolution stating that it would be favourable to a common Council or Conference with other Evangelical Churches, to consult on 'great moral and spiritual questions, and decisions be arrived at for making more effective witness to the Kingdom of God...'.[20] The Church of Ireland-Presbyterian joint co-operating committee decided to postpone any action on this proposal until after the Lambeth Conference of 1920. In 1923 the joint committee of the Presbyterian and Methodist Churches and the joint Committee of the Presbyterian Church and the Church of Ireland developed into United Council of Christian Churches and Religious Communions in

Ireland (which changed its name in 1966 to the Irish Council of Churches).

The next significant ecumenical venture was in 1963 when union talks began between the Methodist, Congregationalist and Presbyterian Churches in Ireland. An invitation was extended to the Church of Ireland, which responded by establishing three sets of bipartite talks. The talks merged in 1968 with the withdrawal of the Congregationalists to form the tripartite talks. In March 1968, a declaration of intent was published, committing to the search for unity, without a predetermined concept of how that unity would come about, and acknowledging that each of the Churches would have to change. They acknowledge the level of agreement on common faith and promote working together 'at all levels, on those things which conviction does not require us to do separately'.[21] In 1973 they produced a major report entitled *Towards a united Church* which set the background to the discussions, highlighted the agreement reached and proposed a new united Church bringing together the major traditions of each of the three Churches involved. The proposals eventually foundered over the concerns of the Presbyterian Church accepting the historic episcopate. In 1978 the Consultation decided to ask the respective Churches for clear terms of reference, by requesting them:

> …to indicate clearly to us if they wish us to formulate proposals for: 1) a full mutual recognition of ministries; 2) a form of federation; [and] 3) organic union.[22]

This was voted upon in the General Synod, General Assembly and Conference the following year. Synod accepted organic union without voting on the other options. The Assembly and Conference voted on all three and the statistics revealed a readiness to a scheme of union. In 1974, the three governing bodies passed the following resolution:

> ...We recognise the ordained ministries of our three Churches as real and efficacious ministries of the word and sacraments through which God's love is proclaimed, his grace mediated, and his fatherly care exercised. We also recognise that our three Churches have different forms of church order and that each of us continues to cherish the forms which we have inherited...[23]

The tripartite consultation acknowledged the readiness to 'recognise the ministries of our three Churches... within the whole body of Christ' without implying a constitutional right to minister in the other churches.[24] The 1974 resolution recognising the ministries of the Presbyterian and Methodist Churches as 'real and efficacious' was a major step for the Church of Ireland whose General Synod had not been prepared to accept a similar proposal in 1935. However the Northern Ireland 'Troubles', among other factors, brought a greater conservatism in the Churches and a political shift to the right, and the enthusiasm for reunion felt in the 1960s slowly died.

Coupled with this was the grant given by the World

Council of Churches (WCC) to the Patriotic Front in former Rhodesia, which came at the same time as the news of the murders of several Northern Ireland missionaries in that country in 1978. A special meeting of the General Assembly of the Presbyterian Church in Ireland was called, and they suspended their membership of the WCC, followed by their withdrawal from the WCC in 1980. Alongside their specific concerns relating to the 'programme to combat racism', there were also underlying conservative theological trends in Irish Presbyterianism that were at variance with WCC theological approaches. The Presbyterian withdrawal from the WCC was followed by its rejection in 1988 of the proposal to form a new tripartite theological working party to succeed the tripartite consultations.

The proposal was, however, accepted by the Church of Ireland and the Methodist Church in Ireland. Following the withdrawal of the Presbyterian Church from the negotiations bipartite talks were established between the Church of Ireland and the Methodist Church in Ireland, which took the form of the Joint Theological Working Party (JTWP) as recommended by the tripartite talks with the following terms of reference:

a) To consider the implications of the work of the tripartite consultation, in the new bilateral context;

b) To relate the work of the Anglican–Methodist International Commission to Anglican–Methodist relations in Ireland;

c) To explore opportunities for developing Church of Ireland–Methodist relationships and to make appropriate recommendations for the furtherance of the visible unity of the Church;

d) To report annually to the two Churches.[25]

After a number of years seeking to discern the way forward, response to the Anglican–Methodist International Commission (AMIC) documents gave the necessary impetus, and, in 1999, the governing bodies were invited to ratify new terms of reference.[26] In doing so they endorsed the measure of agreement reached by JTWP and encouraged it 'to hasten forward with its work'.[27]

5
The Covenant

AT A RESIDENTIAL MEETING, the perspective from which the Joint Theological Working Party (hereafter JTWP) came to see its ongoing work was that of mission. The meeting was attended by the then Primate of All–Ireland, the Most Revd Dr Robin Eames, and the then President of the Methodist Church in Ireland, the Revd Dr Kenneth Wilson. Clearly there was theological difference, but what was paramount in the 'new' Ireland[28] was joint witness to the truths and relevance of the faith. This would be facilitated by a public and formal recognition of what the archbishop of Armagh memorably referred to as 'the special relationship between the two Churches'. A Covenant text, based on the Fetter Lane Declaration of the Church of England and the Moravian Church of Great Britain[29] was drafted.

The Covenant (in both initial draft and final form) opens by affirming what each church can, in good conscience, say about the other in terms of the following:

- unity, holiness, catholicity and apostolicity;
- the sacraments of baptism and Holy Communion;
- the common faith set forth in scripture and summarised in the historic creeds;
- a common inheritance and an acceptable diversity in worship;
- ministry;
- oversight.

It affirms the belief that the Churches are being called into a fuller relationship of commitment to common life and mission and a growing together in unity.

Ten steps are proposed towards that end, of which it might be said that:

Steps 1–5 concern and should be implemented by local circuits and parishes;

Steps 6–9 are more structural and should be implemented by the governing bodies at national level;

Step 10 relates to the ongoing theological dialogue and exploration.

Note that in the text, the concept of mission – the apostolic mission of the whole people of God; a concern for continuity of mission; sharing a common mission; strengthening the mission of the Church; consultation on mission – features prominently.

Process

The Covenant, in draft form, was presented to the General Synod and the Conference in summer 2000. JTWP asked that it be sent to circuits and parishes for response and comment. This was agreed, with the Conference asking that explanatory notes be included.

In the light of these responses, small alterations were made to the text, primarily in the interests of clarification. A revised draft was presented to the General

Synod and the Conference of 2001, urging that 'the journey of exploration be continued'.

The Covenant was presented for a final vote to the General Synod and the Conference in 2002. The Synod, after a very moving discussion, passed the resolution 'to enter into a covenant relationship with the Methodist Church in Ireland' unanimously. Three weeks later, the Methodist Conference passed the same resolution in respect of the Church of Ireland with an overwhelming majority.

The Covenant was formally signed in September 2002, and the JTWP was disbanded after the General Synod and the Conference of 2003, having taken a year to set in place an appropriate implementation body, namely, the Covenant Council.

References

1. D.A.L. Cooney, *The Methodists in Ireland* (2001), p.15
2. R.L.Cole, *A History of Methodists in Dublin* (1932), p.16
3. ibid. p.30
4. F. Jeffrey, *Irish Methodism; an historical account of its traditions, theology and influence* (1964), p. 7
5. D.A.L. Cooney, *The Methodists in Ireland* (2001), p. 34
6. e.g. the Covenants produced in both Ireland and England.
7. e.g. *Sharing in the Apostolic Communion.*
8 J. Wesley, *Letters VII* p.321 (4th March 1784), cited in F. Baker, *John Wesley and the Church of England* (1970), p. 279
9. Cited in B. Tabraham *The making of Methodism* (1995), p. 48
10. John Wesley was aware that there was no single individual whom he considered able to succeed him in the mantle of leadership. In February 1784 he signed a declaratory deed poll, investing 100 named preachers (known as 'The legal hundred') as the legal members of 'The Conference of the People called Methodists', with authority to carry out its specified business. This group in turn became 'Conference', as it is known today.
11. Sermon on 'The ministerial office', cited in F. Baker, *John Wesley and the Church of England* (1970), p. 2
12. J. Wesley, *Journal VII* p. 481-2; *Arminian Magazine* 1797, p. 313, cited in F. Baker, *John Wesley and the Church of England* (1970), pp. 300-1
13. F. Jeffrey, *Irish Methodism; an historical account of its traditions, theology and influence* (1964), pp. 33-4
14. The main body of Methodists from which they seceded were known at this time as Wesleyan Methodists.
15. Statistics from D.A.L. Cooney, *The Methodists in Ireland* (2001), p. 68
16. Cited in R.L. Cole, *History of Methodism in Ireland 1860-1960* (1960), p. 22
17. *Lambeth Conferences 1867-1930*, pp. 119-124
18. *An Anglican-Methodist Covenant: Common statement of the formal conversations between the Methodist Church of Great Britain and the Church of England*, p. 20
19. *The Lambeth Conference 1968*, p. 127

20. Quoted in I.M. Ellis, *Vision and reality: a survey of twentieth-century Irish inter-Church relations* (1992), p. 13
21. Cited in I.M. Ellis, ibid., p. 176
22. *Journal of the General Synod of the Church of Ireland 1978*, p. 161
23. *Journal of the General Synod of the Church of Ireland 1974*, p. 182
24. *The full mutual recognition of ministries*, unpublished Tripartite Consultation document, 1979, cited in I.M. Ellis, *Vision and reality* (1992), p.131
25. Joint Theological Working Party, 'The Church' report *(1995)*
26. These terms of reference were as follows:-

    (a) To examine and express the theological issues involved in the promotion of visible unity between the Methodist Church in Ireland and the Church of Ireland , and make appropriate recommendations;

    (b) To explore opportunities for developing Church of Ireland/Methodist understanding and relationships at all levels, local regional and national;

    (c) To study the work of conversations involving Anglican and Methodist Churches in England, Scotland and Wales, and relate these to the relations between our two churches in Ireland;

    (d) To relate the work of the Anglican/Methodist International Commission and of any other major Methodist/Anglican conversations to the work of JTWP in Ireland;

    (e) To report annually to our two Churches.
27. Methodist Church in Ireland, *Minutes of Conference 1999*, p.83
28. Since 1988 and disbandment of the Tripartite Consultation, many new factors came into play on the Irish scene, and particularly in the Republic of Ireland, where each Church found itself in a minority position (Protestants of all persuasions are considered in total to be 3.5% of the population). Such factors are documented very readably in Mary Kenny, *Goodbye to Catholic Ireland* (London 1997), and included the following:

    ●Two successive Heads of State who have been women….the impact of this on public thinking should not be underestimated;

●The unforeseen events affecting the Roman Catholic Church, including the Bishop Casey affair and a variety of child sexual abuse scandals, the revelations concerning one of which brought down the Irish Government of the day;

●A very rapidly rising tide of secularism.

29. The Fetter Lane Declaration formed the basis for an agreement between the Moravian Church in Ireland and the Church of Ireland Diocese of Connor. Most Irish Moravians live within the geographical area of the Connor Diocese.

Select Bibliography

Books

A. Acheson, *A history of the Church of Ireland 1691-2001* (revised edition, Dublin, 2002)

A. Armstrong, *The Church of England, the Methodists and society 1700-1850* (London, 1973)

F. Baker, *John Wesley and the Church of England* (London, 1970)

R.L. Cole, *A history of Methodists in Dublin* (Dublin, 1932)

R.L. Cole, *History of Methodism in Ireland 1860-1960* (Belfast, 1960)

D.A.L. Cooney, *The Methodists in Ireland; a short history* (Dublin, 2001)

I.M. Ellis, *Vision and reality: a survey of twentieth-century Irish inter-Church relations* (Belfast, 1992)

H. Fey, (ed.),*The ecumenical advance; a history of the ecumenical movement, 2, 1948-1968* (London, 1970)

I.D. Henderson, *The Methodist Conference in Ireland* (revised edition, Donegal, 2001)

F. Jeffrey, *Irish Methodism; an historical account of its traditions, theology and influence* (Belfast, 1964)

N. Lossky, J.M. Bonino, J. Pobee, T.F. Stransky, G. Wainwright & P. Webb (eds.) *Dictionary of the Ecumenical Movement* (Geneva, 1991)

S. Neill, *Anglicanism* (Middlesex, 1962)

J. Pollock, *John Wesley 1703-1791* (London, 1989)

S.G. Poyntz, *Journey towards union – the next stretch of road* (Dublin, 1976)

R. Rouse and S.C. Neill, *History of the ecumenical movement, 1517-1948* (London, 1954, and 2nd edition, London, 1967)

S. Sykes, T*he study of Anglicanism* (revised edition, London, 1998)

B. Tabraham, *The making of Methodism* (London, 1995)

G. Wilson, *The faith of an Anglican* (Glasgow, 1980)

Reports & responses

An Anglican-Methodist Covenant (Methodist Publishing House, and Church House Publishing, London, 2001)

An Anglican-Methodist Covenant: common statement of the formal conversations between the Methodist Church of Great Britain and the Church of England (Church House Publishing, London & Methodist Publishing House, Peterborough, 2001)

Anglican-Methodist Unity, Part 1: the Ordinal. Report of the Anglican-Methodist Unity Commission (London, 1968)

Baptism, Eucharist & Ministry (B.E.M.); Faith & Order Paper no. 111. Produced by the Faith and Order Committee, World Council of Churches (Geneva, 1982)

Church of Ireland / Methodist Church in Ireland, draft Covenant. Produced by the JTWP (July 2000)

Church of Ireland / Methodist Church in Ireland, revised draft Covenant. Produced by the JTWP (2001)

Commitment to Mission and Unity: Report of the informal conversations between the Methodist Church and the Church of England (Church House Publishing, London & Methodist Publishing House, Peterborough, 1996)

Towards a response to commitment for mission and unity. Produced by the Council for Christian Unity of the General Synod of the Church of England. (London, 1997)

Journal of the General Synod of the Church of Ireland (published annually)

Lambeth Conferences, 1867-1930 (London, 1948)

Lambeth Conference 1948, (London, 1948)

Lambeth Conference 1968; resolutions and reports (London & New York, 1968)

Sharing in the Apostolic Communion, interim report (The Anglican Communion & the World Methodist Council, 1993)

Sharing in the Apostolic Communion (The Anglican Communion & the World Methodist Council, 1996)

The Church: A series of Six Studies for use at Local Level. Produced by JTWT (1995)

Websites

The Covenant Council
http://www.covenantcouncil.com/

The Anglican Communion
www.anglicancommunion.org/

The Irish Council of Churches
www.irishchurches.org

The Methodist Church in England
www.methodist.org.uk/

The General Synod of the Church of England
http://england.anglican.org/synod/2003July/

Unpublished manuscripts

Joint Theological Working Party of the Church of Ireland and the Methodist Church in Ireland (JTWP), 'Celebrating the Covenant' (liturgy used at the signing of the Covenant); Minutes of the JTWP meetings, 1990-2002; 'Responses to the Draft Covenant', 2000; 'Sharing in the Apostolic Communion, a response', 1995. Further information about access to these sources is available from the secretary of the Covenant Council.

G.M Kingston, 'Dialogue for the sake of mission': unpublished paper presented to the Oxford Institute of Methodist Studies

P. A. Thompson, 'Methodist-Anglican dialogue in Ireland 1989-2003: the work of the Joint Theological Working Party': unpublished MPhil (Ecumenics) thesis, Irish School of Ecumenics, Trinity College Dublin (2000)